Directing Your Path to Wealth: A simple Guide to Financial Self-sufficiency and a Life of Abundance.

Max Brown

Table of Contents

Introduction
- Welcome to Your Path to Wealth
- The Power of Financial Self-Sufficiency
- Embracing a Life of Abundance

Chapter 1: Building a Strong Foundation
- Understanding Your Current Financial Situation
- Setting Clear Financial Goals
- Creating a Budget That Works for You

Chapter 2: Shifting Your Mindset for Success
- Identifying and Overcoming Limiting Beliefs
- Cultivating an Abundance Mindset
- Harnessing the Power of Positive Thinking

Chapter 3: Practical Strategies for Financial Growth
- Investing in Your Future
- Building Multiple Streams of Income

- Embracing Your Journey to Wealth and Abundance

Introduction:

Welcome to Your Path to Wealth

Welcome to "Directing Your Path to Wealth: A Simple Guide to Financial Self-Sufficiency and a Life of Abundance." In this book, we embark on a transformative journey towards financial empowerment and prosperity. This guide is designed to help you unlock the secrets to building wealth, cultivating a prosperity mindset, and living a life of abundance.

In today's fast-paced and ever-changing world, achieving financial self-sufficiency is more important than ever. The ability to manage your finances effectively, make smart investment decisions, and build a solid financial foundation is key to creating a life of abundance and freedom. This book is your roadmap to achieving these goals and taking control of your financial future.

As we embark into the principles of wealth creation and abundance, it's essential to understand that true wealth goes beyond just money. It encompasses all aspects of
your life, including your health, relationships, personal growth, and overall well-being. By cultivating a holistic approach to wealth, you can create a life that is rich in all areas and experience true fulfillment.

Throughout this book, you will discover practical strategies, proven techniques, and powerful mindset shifts that will empower you to take charge of your financial destiny. From setting clear financial goals to implementing effective money management practices, each chapter is designed to equip you with the tools and knowledge you need to succeed on your path to wealth.

We believe that everyone has the potential to achieve financial independence and create a life of abundance. No matter where you are starting from or what challenges you may be facing, this book is here to guide you towards a brighter financial future. By implementing the principles and practices outlined in these pages, you can pave the way for a more prosperous and fulfilling life.

Our approach is rooted in the belief that abundance is not limited – there is more than enough wealth and prosperity to go around for everyone. By adopting an abundance mindset and embracing the power of positive thinking, you can attract wealth and opportunities into your life with ease. This book will show you how to tap into this universal abundance and create a life that is overflowing with blessings.

As you embark on this journey towards financial self-sufficiency and a life of abundance, remember that you are not alone. We are here to support you every step of the way and provide you with the guidance and encouragement you need to succeed. Together, we can unlock the doors to wealth and prosperity and create a future filled with unlimited possibilities.

Get ready to transform your relationship with money, unleash your full potential, and direct your path to wealth. The journey starts now – are you ready to take the first step towards a life of abundance?

Let's begin this exciting adventure together and create a future filled with prosperity, joy, and fulfillment. Welcome to "Directing Your Path to Wealth" – your guide to financial self-sufficiency and a life of abundance.

The Power of Financial Self-Sufficiency

Financial self-sufficiency is not just about having enough money to cover your expenses – it's about having the freedom and independence to create the life you desire.
When you are financially self-sufficient, you are in control of your financial destiny and can make decisions that align with your values and goals. The power of financial self-sufficiency lies in the ability to live on your own terms, without being dependent on others for your financial well-being.

One of the key benefits of financial self-sufficiency is the sense of security and peace of mind it brings. When you have a solid financial foundation, you can weather unexpected expenses, job loss, or economic downturns with confidence. You are not at the mercy of external forces but instead have the resources and resilience to navigate life's challenges with grace.

Financial self-sufficiency also empowers you to pursue your passions and dreams without limitations. Whether you want to start a business, travel the world, or pursue a creative endeavor, having financial stability gives you the freedom to take risks and explore new opportunities. You no longer have to settle for a life that is dictated by financial constraints but can instead design a life that reflects your true desires and aspirations.

Moreover, financial self-sufficiency allows you to build wealth and create a legacy for future generations. By making smart investment decisions, saving diligently, and living within your means, you can accumulate wealth over time and secure a comfortable future for yourself and your loved ones. You can leave a lasting impact on the world and make a difference in the lives of others through your financial abundance.

Another powerful aspect of financial self-sufficiency is the sense of empowerment and confidence it instills in you. When you are in control of your finances, you can make decisions from a place of strength and clarity, rather than fear or uncertainty. You have the ability to set ambitious goals, take calculated risks, and pursue opportunities that align with your vision for the future.

In essence, financial self-sufficiency is about more than just money – it's about creating a life of abundance, freedom, and fulfillment. It's about taking charge of your financial destiny and directing your path towards a future filled with unlimited possibilities.
 By cultivating a prosperity mindset, embracing smart money management practices, and making intentional choices about how you use your resources, you can unlock the power of financial self-sufficiency and create a life that is rich in all areas.

As you embark on this journey towards financial empowerment and prosperity, remember that the power to create the life you desire lies within you. By harnessing the power of financial self-sufficiency, you can transform your relationship with money, unlock your full potential, and create a future that is overflowing with blessings.

Embracing a Life of Abundance

Living a life of abundance goes beyond material wealth – it's about cultivating a mindset of gratitude, generosity, and fulfillment in all areas of your life. When you embrace a life of abundance, you open yourself up to endless possibilities and create a sense of richness that transcends monetary value.

One key aspect of embracing a life of abundance is practicing gratitude. By focusing on the blessings and abundance already present in your life, you shift your perspective from scarcity to abundance. Gratitude allows you to appreciate the simple joys, moments of connection, and gifts that surround you every day, fostering a sense of contentment and fulfillment.

Another essential element of living abundantly is practicing generosity. When you give freely of your time, resources, and energy to others, you create a ripple effect of positivity and abundance in the world. Generosity not only benefits those you help but also enriches your own life by fostering a sense of connection, purpose, and fulfillment.

Moreover, embracing a life of abundance involves living authentically and aligning your actions with your values and passions. When you pursue activities that bring you joy, engage in meaningful relationships, and follow your heart's desires, you create a life that is rich in purpose and fulfillment. By being true to yourself and honoring your unique gifts and talents, you invite abundance to flow into every aspect of your life.

Furthermore, cultivating a mindset of abundance involves letting go of limiting beliefs, fears, and scarcity mentality that hold you back from embracing all the blessings that life has to offer. By releasing negative patterns of thinking and opening yourself up to new possibilities, you create space for abundance to manifest in unexpected ways.

In essence, embracing a life of abundance is about recognizing the infinite potential within you and aligning with the flow of prosperity and blessings that surround you. By practicing gratitude, generosity, authenticity, and releasing limitations, you can create a life that is overflowing with abundance in all its forms. Are you ready to embrace a life of abundance and unlock the limitless possibilities that await you? The journey towards abundance begins with a single step – are you ready to take that step today?

Chapter 1. Building a Strong Foundation.

Understanding Your Current Financial Situation.

Building a strong foundation for your financial future begins with a clear understanding of your current financial situation in relation to your future desires. By taking a proactive approach to assess where you stand financially, you can create a roadmap that will guide you towards achieving your long-term goals and aspirations.

The first step in understanding your current financial situation is to conduct a thorough assessment of your income, expenses, assets, and liabilities. By creating a detailed budget that outlines your monthly cash flow and financial obligations, you can gain insight into how your money is being spent and identify areas where you can make adjustments to align with your future desires.

Furthermore, it is essential to take stock of your assets, such as savings, investments, and property, as well as your liabilities, including debts and loans. Understanding your net worth – the difference between your assets and liabilities – can provide valuable information about your overall financial health and help you make informed decisions about how to grow your wealth over time.

Once you have a clear picture of your current financial situation, the next step is to define your future desires and set specific, measurable, achievable, relevant, and time-bound (SMART) goals. Whether your goals include buying a home, starting a business, saving for retirement, or traveling the world, having a clear vision of what you want to achieve will help you stay motivated and focused on taking the necessary steps to turn your dreams into reality.

In addition to setting goals, it is crucial to develop a strategic plan that outlines the steps you need to take to reach your desired financial outcomes. This may involve creating a savings plan, investing in assets that align with your long-term objectives, paying off debts, or seeking professional advice from a financial advisor to help you make informed decisions about managing your money effectively.

Moreover, it is essential to regularly review and adjust your financial plan as needed to ensure that you are on track to meet your goals. By monitoring your progress, making necessary changes, and staying disciplined in your financial habits, you can build a strong foundation that will support you in achieving the future desires you have set for yourself.

In conclusion, understanding your current financial situation relative to your future desires is a critical step in building a strong foundation for financial success. By assessing where you stand financially, setting SMART goals, developing a strategic plan, and staying committed to your objectives, you can create a roadmap that will guide you towards achieving the life of abundance and fulfillment that you envision for yourself. Are you ready to take control of your financial future and turn your dreams into reality? Start by understanding where you are today and taking the necessary steps to create the future you desire.

. Setting Clear Financial Goals

Setting clear financial goals is a crucial step in achieving long-term financial success and turning your dreams into reality. By defining specific, measurable, achievable, relevant, and time-bound (SMART) goals, you can create a roadmap that will guide you towards financial independence and fulfillment. Here are some key points to consider when setting clear financial goals:

1. **Define Your Goals**: Start by identifying what you want to achieve financially. Whether your goals include buying a home, saving for retirement, starting a business, or traveling the world, it is essential to have a clear vision of what you want to accomplish. By defining your goals, you can create a sense of purpose and motivation that will drive you towards success.

2. **Make Them SMART:** When setting financial goals, it is important to ensure that they are specific, measurable, achievable, relevant, and time-bound. For example, instead of setting a vague goal like "saving money," a SMART goal would be "saving $10,000 for a down payment on a house within two years." By making your goals

SMART, you can track your progress, stay focused, and hold yourself accountable for achieving them.

3. **Prioritize Your Goals**: It is common to have multiple financial goals, but it is important to prioritize them based on their importance and urgency. Determine which goals are most critical to your long-term financial well-being and focus on achieving those first. By prioritizing your goals, you can allocate your resources effectively and make steady progress towards achieving them.

4. **Break Them Down:** Large financial goals can seem overwhelming, but breaking them down into smaller, manageable tasks can make them more achievable. Create a step-by-step plan that outlines the specific actions you need to take to reach each goal. By breaking down your goals into smaller milestones, you can track your progress and celebrate your achievements along the way.

5. **Review and Adjust**: Regularly review your financial goals to ensure that they are still relevant and aligned with your current circumstances. Life changes, unexpected expenses may arise, or new

opportunities may present themselves. By reviewing and adjusting your goals as needed, you can stay flexible and adapt to changing circumstances while staying focused on your long-term objectives.

In conclusion, setting clear financial goals is a critical step in building a strong foundation for financial success. By defining SMART goals, prioritizing them, breaking them down into manageable tasks, and regularly reviewing and adjusting them as needed, you can create a roadmap that will guide you towards achieving the future you desire. Are you ready to set clear financial goals and take control of your financial future? Start by defining what you want to achieve and taking the necessary steps to turn your dreams into reality.

Creating a Budget That Works for You

Creating a budget that works for you is essential for achieving financial stability and reaching your financial goals. A budget is a plan that helps you track your income and expenses, allowing you to make informed decisions about how to manage your money effectively. Here are some simple steps to help you create a budget that works for you:

1. **Start by tracking your income and expenses**: The first step in creating a budget is to track your income and expenses. Make a list of all your sources of income, including your salary, bonuses, and any other sources of income. Then, track your expenses by keeping a record of all your spending, including bills, groceries, entertainment, and other expenses.

2. **Set your financial goals**: Before creating a budget, it's important to set clear financial goals. Whether you want to save for a vacation, pay off debt, or build an emergency fund, having specific goals will help you stay motivated and focused on your budgeting efforts.

3. **Determine your fixed and variable expenses**: Divide your expenses into fixed and variable categories. Fixed expenses are recurring costs that

stay the same each month, such as rent, mortgage payments, and insurance premiums. Variable expenses, on the other hand, can fluctuate from month to month, such as groceries, entertainment, and dining out.

4. **Create a budget template**: Use a budget template or spreadsheet to organize your income and expenses. List all your sources of income at the top of the sheet and subtract your fixed expenses to determine how much you have left for variable expenses and savings.

5. **Allocate funds for savings and emergencies**: It's important to prioritize saving in your budget. Allocate a portion of your income towards savings goals, such as an emergency fund or retirement savings. Having a financial cushion will help you navigate unexpected expenses without derailing your budget.

6. **Monitor and adjust your budget regularly**: Once you've created a budget, it's important to monitor your spending regularly and make adjustments as needed. Track your expenses

against your budget to ensure you're staying on track with your financial goals. If you find that you're overspending in certain areas, look for ways to cut back or reallocate funds to stay within your budget.

Creating a budget that works for you takes time and effort, but the benefits of financial stability and peace of mind are well worth it. By following these simple steps and staying committed to your budgeting goals, you can take control of your finances and work towards a brighter financial future.

Chapter 2. Shifting Your Mindset for Success.

Identifying and Overcoming Limiting Beliefs.

Identifying and overcoming limiting beliefs is a crucial step in shifting your mindset for success. Limiting beliefs are negative thoughts and beliefs that hold you back from reaching your full potential and achieving your goals. These beliefs often stem from past experiences, societal norms, or self-doubt, and can manifest as thoughts like "I'm not good enough," "I don't deserve success," or "I'll never be able to achieve my dreams."

To identify limiting beliefs, start by paying attention to your inner dialogue and noticing any recurring negative thoughts or self-criticisms. Reflect on where these beliefs might have originated and how they have influenced your actions and decisions. Consider how these beliefs have impacted your confidence, motivation, and willingness to take risks.

Once you've identified your limiting beliefs, it's important to challenge them and replace them with empowering beliefs that support your growth and success. Here are some strategies to help you overcome limiting beliefs:

1. **Reframe negative thoughts**: When you catch yourself thinking a limiting belief, reframe it into a positive affirmation. For example, instead of saying "I'm not smart enough to start my own business," reframe it as "I have the skills and knowledge to succeed in my entrepreneurial ventures."

2. **Seek evidence to counteract limiting beliefs**: Challenge your limiting beliefs by seeking evidence that disproves them. Look for examples of people who have overcome similar challenges or achieved success despite facing similar obstacles.

3. **Practice self-compassion:** Be kind to yourself and practice self-compassion when dealing with limiting beliefs. Treat yourself with the same kindness and understanding you would offer a friend facing similar challenges.

4. **Surround yourself with positive influences**: Surround yourself with supportive and positive influences who uplift and encourage you to challenge your limiting beliefs. Seek out mentors, friends, or resources that inspire and motivate you to reach your full potential.

5. **Take action despite fear**: Overcoming limiting beliefs requires taking action despite fear and self-doubt. Start small by setting achievable goals and gradually expanding your comfort zone. Celebrate your successes along the way to boost your confidence and reinforce positive beliefs about yourself.

By identifying and overcoming limiting beliefs, you can cultivate a growth mindset, build resilience, and unlock your full potential for success.

Cultivating an Abundance Mindset

Cultivating an abundance mindset is a powerful practice that can transform your life and unlock a world of endless possibilities. An abundance mindset is the belief that there is more than enough of everything to go around – whether it's wealth, success, love, or opportunities. By shifting your perspective from scarcity to abundance, you open yourself up to a wealth of positive experiences and opportunities that can lead to greater fulfillment and success.

One key aspect of cultivating an abundance mindset is practicing gratitude. Gratitude is the foundation of abundance, as it allows you to appreciate what you have in the present moment rather than focusing on what you lack. By acknowledging and expressing gratitude for the blessings in your life – no matter how big or small – you invite more positivity and abundance into your life.

Another essential element of an abundance mindset is embracing a growth mindset. A growth mindset is the belief that your abilities and intelligence can be developed through effort and perseverance. By viewing challenges as opportunities for growth and learning, you can overcome obstacles with resilience and determination, ultimately leading to greater success and abundance.

In addition to gratitude and a growth mindset, **cultivating an abundance mindset also involves letting go of limiting beliefs and scarcity mentality**. Limiting beliefs are negative thoughts that hold you back from reaching your full potential, while scarcity mentality is the fear of not having enough or missing out on opportunities. By identifying and challenging these beliefs, you can replace them with empowering thoughts that support your growth and success.

Furthermore, **surrounding yourself with positive influences and like-minded individuals** who uplift and inspire you can help reinforce your abundance mindset. Seek out mentors, friends, and resources that support your vision of abundance and encourage you to dream big and take bold actions towards your goals.

Lastly, **taking inspired action** is essential in cultivating an abundance mindset. Set clear intentions, visualize your goals, and take consistent steps towards manifesting your desires. Trust in the process and believe that the universe is conspiring in your favor to bring abundance into your life.

In conclusion, cultivating an abundance mindset is a transformative practice that can lead to greater fulfillment, success, and joy. By practicing gratitude, embracing a growth mindset, letting go of limiting beliefs, surrounding yourself with positive influences, and taking inspired action, you can create a life filled with abundance and limitless possibilities. Embrace the journey of self-discovery and empowerment as you cultivate an abundance mindset and watch as the universe aligns to bring you all that you desire.

Harnessing the Power of Positive Thinking

Harnessing the power of positive thinking is a transformative practice that can elevate your mindset, enhance your well-being, and unlock a world of endless possibilities. Positive thinking is the belief that you have the power to shape your reality through your thoughts, emotions, and actions. By cultivating a positive mindset, you can attract more positivity into your life, overcome challenges with resilience, and create a life filled with joy, abundance, and success.

One key aspect of harnessing the power of positive thinking is practicing self-awareness and mindfulness. Become aware of your thoughts and emotions, and choose to focus on the positive aspects of any situation. By shifting your perspective from negativity to positivity, you can reframe challenges as opportunities for growth and learning, ultimately leading to greater resilience and emotional well-being.

Another essential element of positive thinking is practicing affirmations and visualization. Affirmations are positive statements that you repeat to yourself to reinforce empowering beliefs and attitudes. By affirming positive thoughts and beliefs about yourself and your life, you can boost your self-confidence, increase your motivation, and attract more positivity into your life. Visualization is another powerful tool that involves mentally picturing yourself achieving your goals and living your desired reality. By visualizing your success and embodying the feelings of accomplishment, you can program your subconscious mind to manifest your desires into reality.

Furthermore, **surrounding yourself with positive influences and like-minded individuals** can help reinforce your positive thinking practice. Seek out mentors, friends, and resources that support your vision of positivity and encourage you to stay focused on your goals. By cultivating a supportive environment filled with optimism and encouragement, you can amplify the power of positive thinking in your life.

In addition, **taking inspired action is crucial in harnessing the power of positive thinking**. Set clear intentions, create actionable goals, and take consistent steps towards manifesting your dreams. Trust in the process and believe in your ability to create the life you desire through the power of positive thinking.

In conclusion, harnessing the power of positive thinking is a life-changing practice that can lead to greater happiness, success, and fulfillment. By practicing self-awareness, affirmations, visualization, surrounding yourself with positive influences, and taking inspired action, you can cultivate a positive mindset that empowers you to create the life of your dreams. Embrace the power of positive thinking and watch as your reality transforms into a beautiful reflection of your inner positivity and limitless potential.

Chapter 3. Practical Strategies for Financial Growth.

Investing in Your. Future

Investing in your future is not just a choice—it's an unavoidable task that holds the key to unlocking a world of opportunities, growth, and prosperity. In today's ever-changing world, the importance of investing in your future cannot be overstated. Whether it's through education, career development, financial planning, or personal growth, making strategic investments in yourself and your future is essential for long-term success and fulfillment.

One of the most impactful ways to invest in your future is through education and continuous learning. In a rapidly evolving job market where new skills and knowledge are constantly in demand, staying relevant and competitive requires a commitment to lifelong learning. By pursuing higher education, attending workshops and seminars, or acquiring new certifications, you can expand your skill set, enhance your expertise, and position yourself for career advancement and opportunities for growth.

Financial planning is another critical aspect of investing in your future. Building a solid financial foundation through saving, investing, and smart money management is essential for achieving long-term financial security and independence. By setting financial goals, creating a budget, and making informed investment decisions, you can secure your financial future, build wealth, and achieve financial freedom.

Investing in your future also involves taking care of your physical, mental, and emotional well-being. Prioritizing self-care, maintaining a healthy lifestyle, and nurturing positive relationships are all investments that contribute to your overall well-being and happiness. By investing in your health and wellness, you can enhance your quality of life, increase your resilience to challenges, and enjoy a more fulfilling and balanced existence.

Furthermore, investing in your future means setting goals, creating a vision for your life, and taking intentional steps to turn your dreams into reality. By setting clear objectives, developing a plan of action, and staying focused on your goals, you can create a roadmap for success and make progress towards achieving your aspirations. Embracing a growth mindset, staying adaptable to change, and being open to new opportunities are all essential components of investing in your future and seizing the possibilities that lie ahead.

In conclusion, investing in your future is not just a task—it's a mindset, a commitment, and a way of life that empowers you to create the future you desire. By making strategic investments in yourself, your education, your finances, and your well-being, you can pave the way for a brighter tomorrow filled with endless possibilities and opportunities for growth. Embrace the journey of investing in your future with determination, courage, and optimism, knowing that each investment you make today is a stepping stone towards a more fulfilling and prosperous tomorrow.

Building Multiple Streams of Income

Building multiple streams of income is a strategic approach to financial planning that involves diversifying your sources of revenue to create a more stable and resilient income portfolio. By generating income from various sources, individuals can not only increase their overall earnings but also reduce their financial risks and enhance their financial security. This concept of creating multiple streams of income is not only a smart financial strategy but also a key to unlocking new opportunities for growth and prosperity.

One of the primary benefits of building multiple streams of income is the potential to expand your overall earnings. By diversifying your sources of revenue, you can tap into different income streams that complement each other and contribute to your total income. This can include earning money from a full-time job, side hustles, rental properties, investments, freelance work, or any other income-generating activities. By leveraging multiple income streams, you can increase your earning potential, boost your cash flow, and achieve financial stability and independence.

Moreover, building multiple streams of income is also an effective way to reduce financial risks and protect yourself against unexpected downturns or setbacks. Relying on a single source of income, such as a job or business, exposes you to the risk of losing that income if circumstances change, such as a job loss, economic recession, or industry disruption. By diversifying your income sources, you can spread out your risk and safeguard yourself against potential financial shocks. If one income stream falters, you can rely on other sources of revenue to sustain you during challenging times.

In addition to expanding your income and reducing risk, building multiple streams of income also opens up new opportunities for personal and professional growth. By exploring different income-generating activities, you can discover new skills, interests, and passions that can lead to exciting career opportunities or entrepreneurial ventures. Diversifying your income streams can also provide you with a sense of financial freedom, flexibility, and autonomy, allowing you to pursue your goals and dreams without being solely dependent on a single source of income.

In conclusion, building multiple streams of income is a powerful strategy for expanding your earnings, reducing financial risks, and unlocking new opportunities for growth and prosperity. By diversifying your sources of revenue through various income-generating activities, you can create a more stable and resilient financial foundation that empowers you to achieve your financial goals and secure your future. Embrace the concept of building multiple streams of income as a means of enhancing your financial well-being, pursuing your passions, and creating a life of abundance and fulfillment.

Maximizing Your Savings Potential

Maximizing Your Savings Potential:

Investing in High-Yielding and Less Risky Ventures

Saving money is a fundamental aspect of financial planning, but simply stashing your cash in a savings account may not be enough to help you achieve your long-term financial goals. To truly maximize your savings potential, it's essential to consider investing your money in high-yielding and less risky ventures that can generate significant returns while safeguarding your hard-earned money.

One effective way to make your savings work harder for you is to explore investment opportunities that offer attractive returns without exposing you to excessive risks. This can include investing in diversified portfolios of stocks, bonds, mutual funds, or exchange-traded funds (ETFs) that have the potential to deliver solid returns over time. By diversifying your investments across different asset classes and sectors, you can reduce your exposure to market volatility and enhance the overall performance of your investment portfolio.

Another option to consider is investing in real estate, which can provide steady rental income and potential capital appreciation over the long term. Real estate investments, such as rental properties or real estate investment trusts (REITs), offer the opportunity to generate passive income while benefiting from the appreciation of property values. By carefully selecting properties in desirable locations and managing them effectively, you can create a reliable income stream and build wealth through real estate investments.

Furthermore, you may also explore alternative investment options, such as peer-to-peer lending, crowdfunding, or investing in small businesses or startups. These alternative investments can offer higher returns than traditional savings accounts or CDs while diversifying your investment portfolio and potentially reducing risk. However, it's important to conduct thorough research, assess the risks involved, and seek professional advice before venturing into alternative investments to ensure that they align with your financial goals and risk tolerance.

In addition to investing in high-yielding ventures, it's crucial to prioritize building an emergency fund to cover unexpected expenses and unforeseen emergencies. Having a cash reserve equivalent to three to six months' worth of living expenses can provide a financial safety net and protect you from having to dip into your investments or incur debt during challenging times.

In conclusion, maximizing your savings potential involves strategically allocating your savings to high-yielding and less risky ventures that can help you grow your wealth over time. By exploring investment opportunities that offer attractive returns, diversifying your portfolio, and maintaining a solid emergency fund, you can make the most of your savings and work towards achieving your financial goals with confidence and peace of mind. Remember to stay informed, seek professional advice when needed, and continuously review and adjust your investment strategy to ensure that it remains aligned with your financial objectives and risk tolerance.

Chapter 4.Inspiring Stories of Wealth and Abundance

Real-Life Examples of Success

Real-Life Examples of Success: Inspiring Stories of Wealth and Abundance

Success comes in many forms, and real-life examples of individuals who have achieved wealth and abundance can serve as powerful sources of inspiration and motivation for those seeking to emulate their success. From humble beginnings to extraordinary achievements, these inspiring stories showcase the resilience, determination, and innovative thinking that have propelled these individuals to financial success. Here are a few unique and noteworthy examples of real-life success stories that are worthy of emulation:

1. **Oprah Winfrey**: From a challenging childhood marked by poverty and abuse, Oprah Winfrey rose to become one of the most influential media moguls in the world. Through hard work, perseverance, and a commitment to empowering others, Oprah built a media empire that includes television shows, magazines, and a successful production company. Her philanthropic efforts have also made a significant impact on education, healthcare, and empowerment initiatives, demonstrating the power of using wealth for positive change.

2. **Warren Buffett**: Known as one of the most successful investors of all time, Warren Buffett started his journey to wealth by investing in stocks at a young age. Through disciplined investing strategies, a keen eye for value, and a long-term perspective, Buffett grew his investment firm, Berkshire Hathaway, into a multinational conglomerate with a diverse portfolio of businesses.

His simple yet effective investment philosophy has inspired countless investors to adopt a patient and rational approach to wealth-building.

3. **Sara Blakely:** As the founder of Spanx, Sara Blakely revolutionized the shapewear industry and became the youngest self-made female billionaire in the world. Starting with just $5,000 in savings and a bold idea, Blakely built her brand from the ground up through creativity, determination, and relentless pursuit of her vision. Her story exemplifies the power of entrepreneurship, innovation, and resilience in overcoming challenges and achieving extraordinary success.

4. **Elon Musk:** A visionary entrepreneur and innovator, Elon Musk has founded several groundbreaking companies, including SpaceX, Tesla, and Neuralink. Through his bold vision for the future of space exploration, sustainable energy, and artificial intelligence, Musk has disrupted multiple industries and pushed the boundaries of what is possible. His relentless drive, risk-taking mentality, and commitment to solving global

challenges have made him a role model for aspiring entrepreneurs and changemakers.

These real-life examples of success demonstrate that wealth and abundance can be achieved through hard work, perseverance, innovation, and a strong sense of purpose. By studying the journeys of these remarkable individuals and learning from their experiences, aspiring entrepreneurs and investors can gain valuable insights into how to navigate challenges, seize opportunities, and create lasting impact through their endeavors. Emulating the qualities of determination, resilience, creativity, and vision exhibited by these successful individuals can inspire others to pursue their own paths to financial success and make a meaningful difference in the world.

In conclusion, real-life success stories serve as powerful reminders that wealth and abundance are attainable goals for those who are willing to dream big, work hard, and stay committed to their visions. By drawing inspiration from these exceptional individuals and applying their lessons to our own pursuits, we can unlock our full potential, achieve financial success, and make a positive impact on the world around us. Let these inspiring stories be a beacon of hope and motivation for all who aspire to create their own paths to wealth and abundance.

Lessons Learned from Financial Trailblazers

Financial trailblazers are individuals who have achieved remarkable success in the world of finance, leaving a lasting impact on the industry and inspiring others to follow in their footsteps. By studying the journeys of these trailblazers, we can uncover valuable lessons that can help us navigate the complex landscape of finance, make informed decisions, and achieve sustainable profitability. Here are some key lessons learned from financial trailblazers that are both acceptable and profitable:

1. **Value Long-Term Relationships**: Financial trailblazers understand the importance of building and nurturing long-term relationships with clients, partners, and stakeholders. By prioritizing trust, transparency, and integrity in all interactions, they create a solid foundation for sustainable growth and

profitability. Cultivating strong relationships based on mutual respect and shared goals can lead to repeat business, referrals, and a loyal customer base that drives long-term success.

2. **Embrace Innovation and Adaptability**: Financial trailblazers are known for their innovative thinking and willingness to embrace change. In a rapidly evolving industry, the ability to adapt to new technologies, market trends, and regulatory changes is essential for staying ahead of the curve and seizing opportunities for growth. By fostering a culture of innovation, experimentation, and continuous learning, trailblazers can identify emerging trends, anticipate challenges, and pivot quickly to capitalize on new opportunities.

3. **Manage Risk Wisely:** Successful financial trailblazers understand the importance of managing risk effectively to protect their investments and ensure long-term profitability. By conducting thorough research, diversifying their portfolios, and implementing risk management strategies, they can mitigate potential losses and maximize returns. Balancing risk and reward, maintaining a disciplined

approach to investment decisions, and staying informed about market conditions are key principles that guide their financial success.

4. **Focus on Value Creation:** Financial trailblazers prioritize value creation over short-term gains, seeking to deliver tangible benefits to their clients, investors, and stakeholders. By identifying opportunities to add value, solve problems, and meet the needs of their target audience, they can build a reputation for excellence and attract a loyal following. By focusing on creating value through innovative products, services, and solutions, trailblazers can differentiate themselves in a competitive market and drive sustainable growth.

5. **Give Back to Society:** Financial trailblazers recognize the importance of giving back to society and making a positive impact on the communities in which they operate. By supporting philanthropic initiatives, social causes, and environmental sustainability efforts, they demonstrate a commitment to corporate social responsibility and ethical business practices. By aligning their financial success with social impact, trailblazers can

build trust, loyalty, and goodwill among stakeholders while contributing to a more sustainable and equitable society.

In conclusion, the lessons learned from financial trailblazers emphasize the importance of building long-term relationships, embracing innovation, managing risk wisely, focusing on value creation, and giving back to society. By incorporating these principles into our own financial strategies and decision-making processes, we can emulate the success of trailblazers and achieve sustainable profitability while maintaining ethical standards and making a positive impact on the world around us. Let these lessons serve as guiding principles as we navigate the complexities of finance and strive to create a more prosperous and inclusive future for all.

How You Can Apply Their Strategies to Your Journey

Applying the strategies of financial trailblazers to your own journey can pave the way for success and sustainable profitability in the world of finance. By incorporating key principles such as building long-term relationships, embracing innovation, managing risk wisely, focusing on value creation, and giving back to society, you can chart a course towards achieving your financial goals and making a positive impact on the industry. Here are some practical ways you can apply their strategies to your journey and increase your chances of success:

1. **Build Strong Relationships:** Focus on cultivating long-term relationships with clients, partners, and stakeholders based on trust, transparency, and integrity. By prioritizing open communication, delivering on promises, and consistently adding value to your interactions, you can build a loyal customer base that drives sustainable growth and profitability.

2. **Embrace Innovation:** Stay informed about emerging technologies, market trends, and regulatory changes in the finance industry. By adopting a mindset of innovation, experimentation, and continuous learning, you can identify opportunities for growth, anticipate challenges, and

pivot quickly to capitalize on new trends and developments.

3. **Manage Risk Effectively:** Conduct thorough research, diversify your investments, and implement risk management strategies to protect your assets and maximize returns. By balancing risk and reward, maintaining a disciplined approach to decision-making, and staying informed about market conditions, you can mitigate potential losses and position yourself for long-term success.

4. **Focus on Value Creation**: Identify opportunities to add value, solve problems, and meet the needs of your target audience. By delivering innovative products, services, and solutions that address market demands and create tangible benefits for your clients, you can differentiate yourself in a competitive landscape and attract a loyal following.

5. **Give Back to Society:** Support philanthropic initiatives, social causes, and environmental sustainability efforts to demonstrate your commitment to corporate social responsibility and ethical business practices. By aligning your

financial success with social impact, you can build trust, loyalty, and goodwill among stakeholders while contributing to a more sustainable and equitable society.

By applying these strategies to your own journey in finance, you can emulate the success of financial trailblazers and increase your chances of achieving sustainable profitability while making a positive impact on the industry and society as a whole. Let these principles guide your decision-making processes and shape your approach to building a successful and fulfilling career in finance.

Chapter 5. Visualization Techniques for Manifesting Wealth

The Power of Visualization in Achieving Your Goals

Visualization is a powerful tool that can help you achieve your goals, including manifesting wealth.

By creating a clear mental image of what you want to achieve, you can harness the power of your mind to bring your desires into reality. The key to successful visualization lies in the details and emotions you infuse into your mental images.

When you visualize your goals, it's essential to be as specific as possible. Instead of simply imagining yourself as wealthy, try to paint a detailed picture of what that wealth looks like for you. Visualize the lifestyle you want to lead, the possessions you want to acquire, and the experiences you want to enjoy. By getting specific about your desires, you create a clear roadmap for your subconscious mind to follow.

In addition to specificity, it's crucial to infuse your visualizations with emotion. The more strongly you can feel the joy, excitement, and gratitude associated with achieving your goals, the more powerful your visualizations will be. Emotions act as a magnet, drawing your desires towards you and helping you align your thoughts and actions with your goals.

Visualizing your goals regularly is another key aspect of harnessing the power of visualization. By incorporating visualization into your daily routine, you keep your goals at the forefront of your mind and maintain a strong connection to your desires. Whether you visualize through meditation, vision boards, or simply daydreaming, consistency is key to reprogramming your subconscious mind and aligning yourself with the energy of abundance.

Furthermore, visualization can help you overcome limiting beliefs and self-doubt that may be holding you back from achieving your goals. By consistently visualizing yourself as successful and abundant, you can rewire your subconscious mind to believe in your own potential and capabilities. As you build confidence in your ability to manifest wealth, you'll find yourself taking inspired action towards your goals with a newfound sense of purpose and determination.

In conclusion, the power of visualization in achieving your goals cannot be overstated. By getting specific, infusing your visualizations with emotion, practicing regularly, and using visualization to overcome limiting beliefs, you can tap into the unlimited potential of your mind and create the life of abundance you desire. Remember, the key to successful visualization lies in believing in the power of your own thoughts and emotions to shape your reality. So start visualizing your dreams today and watch as the universe conspires to make them a reality.

Guided Exercises to Attract Financial Abundance and Stability

Achieving financial abundance and stability is a goal that many people strive for, but it can sometimes feel out of reach. However, with the right mindset and tools, you can attract wealth and prosperity into your life. Guided exercises are a powerful way to focus your energy and intentions towards manifesting financial abundance. Here are some unique and instructive exercises to help you attract wealth and stability:

1. **Gratitude Journaling**: Start by creating a gratitude journal specifically focused on your

financial situation. Each day, take a few minutes to write down three things you are grateful for in relation to your finances. This could be anything from a small windfall to a successful investment decision. By focusing on what you already have, you open yourself up to receiving more abundance in the future.

2. **Visualization Meditation:** Find a quiet space where you won't be disturbed and close your eyes. Take a few deep breaths to center yourself, then visualize your ideal financial situation. Imagine yourself surrounded by wealth, feeling the emotions of joy, gratitude, and abundance. Picture yourself achieving your financial goals and living the life of your dreams. Spend at least 10-15 minutes in this visualization meditation every day to align your energy with your desires.

3. **Affirmation Practice:** Create a set of positive affirmations focused on financial abundance and stability. Repeat these affirmations daily, either out loud or in your mind. Some examples of affirmations include "I am a magnet for wealth and prosperity," "Money flows easily and effortlessly into

my life," and "I am financially secure and stable."
By consistently affirming these positive beliefs, you
reprogram your subconscious mind to attract wealth
into your life.

4. **Money Mindset Reflection**: Take some time to
reflect on your beliefs and attitudes towards money.
Are there any limiting beliefs or negative thoughts
that are holding you back from achieving financial
abundance? Identify these beliefs and work on
replacing them with positive, empowering thoughts.
Remember that you are deserving of wealth and
prosperity, and that abundance is your birthright.

5. **Financial Goal Setting**: Set clear, achievable
financial goals for yourself. Write down your short-
term and long-term financial objectives, along with
specific action steps to help you reach them.
Regularly review your goals and track your
progress towards them. By setting clear intentions
and taking consistent action, you signal to the
universe that you are serious about attracting
financial abundance into your life.

In conclusion, guided exercises can be powerful tools to help you attract financial abundance and stability. By incorporating practices such as gratitude journaling, visualization meditation, affirmations, money mindset reflection, and goal setting into your daily routine, you can align your energy with your desires and manifest the wealth you seek. Remember that consistency, belief, and intention are key to successfully attracting financial abundance into your life. Start practicing these exercises today and watch as the universe conspires to bring you the prosperity and stability you deserve.

Creating a Vision Board for Your Ideal Life

Creating a vision board is a powerful tool that can help you manifest your ideal life by visually representing your goals, dreams, and aspirations. A vision board is a collage of images, words, and affirmations that reflect the life you desire to create. By focusing on these visual representations regularly, you can align your energy with your intentions and attract the experiences and opportunities that will help you achieve your goals. Here are some tips for creating a vision board for your ideal life:

1. **Set Your Intentions**: Before you start creating your vision board, take some time to reflect on what you truly desire in all areas of your life – career, relationships, health, finances, personal growth, etc. Set clear intentions for each area and visualize yourself living your ideal life. This will help you choose images and words that resonate with your goals and aspirations.

2. **Gather Materials**: Collect magazines, newspapers, photos, quotes, and any other materials that inspire you and reflect your vision for the future. You can also print images from the internet or use personal photos that hold special meaning for you. Choose a variety of images and words that evoke positive emotions and align with your intentions.

3. **Create Your Board**: Get a large poster board, corkboard, or canvas to serve as the base for your

vision board. Arrange your chosen images and words on the board in a way that feels visually appealing to you. You can organize them by category or simply place them intuitively. Be creative and trust your instincts as you bring your vision to life.

4. **Visualize and Affirm**: Once your vision board is complete, place it in a prominent location where you will see it every day – such as your bedroom, office, or meditation space. Spend a few minutes each day looking at your vision board, visualizing yourself living the life you desire, and reciting affirmations that support your goals. This practice will help reinforce your intentions and keep you focused on manifesting your ideal life.

5. **Take Inspired Action**: While visualization and affirmation are important components of manifesting your ideal life, it's also essential to take inspired action towards your goals. Use your vision board as a source of motivation and inspiration to guide your decisions and actions. Trust that the universe will support you in achieving your dreams as long as you stay aligned with your vision.

In conclusion, creating a vision board is a fun and effective way to clarify your goals, visualize your ideal life, and manifest the future you desire. By regularly engaging with your vision board and staying focused on your intentions, you can attract the experiences and opportunities that will help you turn your dreams into reality. Start creating your vision board today and watch as your ideal life begins to unfold before your eyes.

Chapter 6. Personal Development Tools for Lasting Success

Goal-Setting Techniques for Long-Term Growth

Goal-setting is a fundamental practice in personal development that can pave the way for lasting success and long-term growth. By setting clear, specific, and achievable goals, you can create a roadmap for your future and propel yourself towards the life you desire. Here are some goal-setting techniques that can help you achieve sustainable growth and fulfillment:

1. **Define Your Vision:** Before setting any goals, take the time to clarify your vision for the future. What do you truly want to achieve in all areas of your life – career, relationships, health, finances, personal growth? Paint a vivid picture of your ideal life and use this vision as a guiding light for setting your goals.

2. **Set SMART Goals**: The SMART criteria – Specific, Measurable, Achievable, Relevant, Time-bound – can help you create goals that are clear, realistic, and actionable. Instead of setting vague goals like "be more successful," break them down into specific objectives with measurable outcomes and a realistic timeline for achievement.

3. **Prioritize Your Goals**: It's essential to prioritize your goals based on their importance and impact on your overall vision. Focus on a few key goals at a time to avoid feeling overwhelmed and increase your chances of success. Identify which goals will

have the most significant positive effect on your life and start with those.

4. **Create Action Plans**: Once you've set your goals, develop detailed action plans that outline the steps you need to take to achieve them. Break down each goal into smaller tasks and establish deadlines for each step. This will help you stay organized, motivated, and accountable throughout the goal-setting process.

5. **Track Your Progress**: Regularly monitor your progress towards your goals to stay on track and make adjustments as needed. Keep a journal, use a goal-tracking app, or create visual progress charts to visualize your achievements and celebrate your successes along the way. This will boost your motivation and momentum towards long-term growth.

6. **Stay Flexible and Adapt**: Life is unpredictable, and circumstances may change along your journey towards your goals. Be flexible and willing to adapt your plans as needed to overcome obstacles and seize new opportunities. Embrace challenges as

learning experiences that can lead to personal growth and resilience.

7. **Practice Self-Reflection**: Take time to reflect on your goals, progress, and experiences regularly. Ask yourself what is working well, what needs improvement, and how you can adjust your approach to align with your long-term growth objectives. Self-reflection can provide valuable insights and help you stay focused on your path to success.

In conclusion, goal-setting techniques are powerful tools for achieving lasting success and personal growth. By defining your vision, setting SMART goals, prioritizing effectively, creating action plans, tracking progress, staying flexible, and practicing self-reflection, you can cultivate a mindset of continuous improvement and propel yourself towards the life of your dreams. Start implementing these techniques today and watch as you embark on a journey of long-term growth and fulfillment.

Self-Care Practices to Support Your Well-being

Self-care practices are essential for supporting your overall well-being and maintaining a healthy balance in your life. Taking care of yourself physically, mentally, and emotionally can help you reduce stress, improve your mood, boost your energy levels, and enhance your quality of life. Here are some self-care practices that you can incorporate into your daily routine to support your well-being:

1. **Mindful Breathing Exercises**: Practice deep breathing exercises to calm your mind, reduce anxiety, and increase your focus. Take a few minutes each day to sit quietly, close your eyes, and focus on your breath. Inhale deeply through your nose, hold for a few seconds, and exhale slowly through your mouth. Repeat this process several times to center yourself and promote relaxation.

2. **Gratitude Journaling**: Start a gratitude journal to cultivate a positive mindset and appreciate the good things in your life. Each day, write down three things you are grateful for, no matter how big or small. Reflecting on the positive aspects of your life can shift your perspective, increase your happiness levels, and boost your overall well-being.

3. **Creative Expression**: Engage in creative activities such as painting, writing, dancing, or playing music to express yourself and relieve stress. Creativity can be a powerful outlet for emotions, allowing you to channel your thoughts and feelings in a constructive way. Experiment with different forms of creative expression to discover what brings you joy and fulfillment.

4. **Digital Detox**: Take regular breaks from screens and technology to reduce mental clutter, improve focus, and recharge your energy. Disconnect from electronic devices for an hour each day and engage in offline activities such as reading a book, going for a walk in nature, or spending time with loved ones. Unplugging can help you reconnect with yourself and prioritize self-care.

5. **Mindful Eating:** Practice mindful eating by savoring each bite, paying attention to your hunger cues, and choosing nourishing foods that support your well-being. Avoid eating on the go or while distracted by screens, and instead focus on enjoying your meals in a peaceful environment. Mindful eating can help you develop a healthier relationship with food and enhance your overall wellness.

6. **Physical Activity**: Incorporate regular physical activity into your routine to boost your mood, increase energy levels, and improve your physical health. Find activities that you enjoy, whether it's yoga, running, dancing, or hiking, and make time for exercise each day. Moving your body can release endorphins, reduce stress, and support your overall well-being.

7. **Self-Compassion Practices**: Practice self-compassion by treating yourself with kindness, understanding, and acceptance. Be gentle with yourself when facing challenges or setbacks, and avoid self-criticism or negative self-talk. Cultivate

self-compassion through affirmations, self-care rituals, and acts of self-love that nurture your inner well-being.

In conclusion, self-care practices are essential for supporting your well-being and maintaining a healthy balance in all areas of your life. By incorporating mindful breathing exercises, gratitude journaling, creative expression, digital detox, mindful eating, physical activity, and self-compassion practices into your daily routine, you can prioritize self-care and enhance your overall wellness. Experiment with these unique and interactive self-care practices to discover what works best for you and create a sustainable self-care routine that supports your long-term well-being.

Cultivating a Balanced Life of Wealth and Fulfilment

Cultivating a balanced life of wealth and fulfillment involves finding harmony between financial success and personal well-being. While wealth can provide material comfort and security, true fulfillment comes from a sense of purpose, meaning, and overall happiness in life. By integrating both aspects, individuals can create a more holistic and enriching lifestyle that promotes long-term satisfaction and well-being.

One key aspect of cultivating a balanced life of wealth and fulfillment is defining your values and priorities. Take the time to reflect on what truly matters to you, whether it's spending time with loved ones, pursuing meaningful work, contributing to your community, or achieving personal growth. By aligning your actions and decisions with your values, you can create a sense of purpose and direction that goes beyond financial success.

Another important element is practicing gratitude and contentment. While striving for financial success is important, it's also essential to appreciate and be grateful for what you already have. Cultivating a mindset of gratitude can help you focus on the positive aspects of your life, foster a sense of contentment, and reduce the constant desire for more material possessions. By acknowledging and appreciating the abundance in your life, you can cultivate a deeper sense of fulfillment that goes beyond monetary wealth.

Furthermore, **maintaining a healthy work-life balance is crucial for overall well-being.** While pursuing financial success is important, it's equally essential to prioritize self-care, relationships, hobbies, and leisure activities. Balancing work commitments with personal time can help prevent burnout, reduce stress, and enhance overall happiness. By setting boundaries, prioritizing self-care, and making time for activities that bring you joy, you can create a more balanced and fulfilling life.

In addition, giving back to others and contributing to causes you care about can also enhance your sense of fulfillment. Whether through volunteering, charitable donations, or acts of kindness, contributing to the well-being of others can bring a sense of purpose and fulfillment that goes beyond personal gain. By making a positive impact on your community or society at large, you can cultivate a deeper sense of meaning and fulfillment in your life.

Overall, cultivating a balanced life of wealth and fulfillment involves integrating financial success with personal well-being, values, gratitude, work-life balance, and giving back to others. By prioritizing these elements and creating a lifestyle that aligns with your values and priorities, you can achieve a more holistic and fulfilling life that promotes long-term happiness and well-being. Strive to find harmony between wealth and personal fulfillment to create a balanced and meaningful life that brings you joy and satisfaction.

Conclusion:

Taking actions towards your financial dreams is a journey that requires dedication, perseverance, and a clear vision of what you want to achieve. It involves setting specific goals, creating a plan, and taking consistent steps to move closer to your desired financial future. By committing to your financial dreams and taking proactive steps to make them a reality, you can create a more secure and fulfilling life for yourself and your loved ones.

One of the first steps towards achieving your financial dreams is to define what success looks like for you. Whether it's buying a home, starting a business, saving for retirement, or traveling the world, having a clear vision of your financial goals can provide you with the motivation and direction needed to take action. By setting specific, measurable, achievable, relevant, and time-bound (SMART) goals, you can create a roadmap that guides your actions and keeps you focused on your objectives.

Once you have defined your financial dreams, the next step is to create a plan that outlines how you will achieve them. This may involve budgeting, saving, investing, paying off debt, increasing your income, or seeking professional advice. By developing a strategic plan that aligns with your goals and resources, you can make informed decisions that support your long-term financial success.

Taking action towards your financial dreams also requires discipline and commitment. It may involve making sacrifices, delaying gratification, and staying focused on your goals even when faced with challenges or setbacks. By cultivating good financial habits, such as living within your means, saving regularly, and investing wisely, you can build a solid foundation for achieving your dreams and creating a more stable financial future.

Moreover, seeking continuous learning and growth in the realm of personal finance can also help you make informed decisions and adapt to changing circumstances. By staying informed about financial trends, strategies, and opportunities, you can enhance your financial literacy and make smarter choices that support your long-term goals.

In conclusion, taking actions towards your financial dreams is a transformative journey that empowers you to create a life of abundance, security, and fulfillment. By setting clear goals, creating a strategic plan, staying disciplined, and seeking continuous growth, you can move closer to realizing your financial aspirations and building a brighter future for yourself and those you care about. Embrace the journey towards your financial dreams with determination, resilience, and a commitment to creating the life you envision.

Embracing Your Journey to Wealth and Abundance is a transformative path that empowers you to shape a future filled with financial security and fulfillment. By setting clear goals, creating a strategic plan, and committing to taking consistent actions, you can pave the way towards achieving your dreams and building a life of abundance.

To embark on this journey, start by defining your financial aspirations and envisioning the life you desire. Set specific, measurable goals that align with your values and priorities, and create a roadmap that outlines the steps you need to take to reach them. Whether it's saving for a dream home, starting a business, or securing your retirement, having a clear vision will guide your actions and keep you focused on your objectives.

Next, cultivate good financial habits such as budgeting, saving, investing wisely, and seeking opportunities for growth and learning. Stay disciplined, resilient, and committed to your goals even in the face of challenges or setbacks. Remember that every small step you take towards your dreams brings you closer to the life of abundance you envision.

In embracing your journey to wealth and abundance, remember that you have the power to shape your financial future and create the life you desire. Take control of your finances, seek knowledge, and stay committed to your goals. The time to start is now. Take action today and embark on the path towards realizing your dreams of wealth and abundance. Your future self will thank you for it.